Love Letters from Asia

Also by Sandra Hochman

Voyage Home

Manhattan Pastures

The Vaudeville Marriage

Love Letters from Asia

poems by

Sandra Hochman

New York · The Viking Press

"This Afternoon," "The Goldfish Wife," "The In-
heritance," "The Central Market," "Secrets," and
"The Storm" originally appeared in *The New
Yorker*. "The Spy" and "Living without Treasures"
originally appeared in *Poetry*. Certain of these
poems first appeared in *Atlantic Monthly, Bard
College Quarterly Review, Bennington Review,
Harper's Bazaar,* and *The Nation.*

To Harvey

Contents

Love Letters from Asia

A Winter Wedding

It's the first day,
A holy day,
As stepping stones
From space slip
Out of their old
Foundations and
We hear them
Fall in the hallways.
Stars
Throb and explode
Near the Spinning Twins.
The brightest
Are *Giants,*
The faintest,
Called *Dwarfs.*

We slide out of the night's path,
And listen to our voices,
Move from
Dipper to Dipper,
On this first,
This holy night
When we march in the great tears,
Down the light corridors.

Here comes the royal family—
Stars whose names
Come from Ethiopia.
We, waiting
At the top of sleep,
Are calling *yes, yes.*

Celebrating Lilies

I have made love to the yellow lilies,
Turned my face against their cool skin,
Led my lips and eyes to their stamens
While I cried to see anything as bright
As these golden lilies.
How I look for them!

There are people who do not explore the in-
Side of flowers, kissing them,
Resting their own tongues on their petals.
I must tell them. Where will I begin?

And I love
Earth, violently, and vegetables,
Stars, and all things that will not break.
My hair smells of melons, marl, jasmine.

The Tennis Master

This ancient Chinese man with white,
Blue, and red striped socks, white
Shorts, hat, white hair, old skin,
Moves quickly on the court,
Looks across the net, and says
"Each time you move your racquet
It is
The closing of a door. Lifting
The racquet, moving it across
Your chest, across your heart—
The closing of a door.
The closing of a door."

I move across the grass,
Awkward, unathletic,
Thinking of the past.

As the swift game continues
I drive strokes past
Camps and boarding schools,
Japan, three years in France,
All the voices
In the flame trees saying,
Love me. Use me. Use me
To see everything, as
One by one
My ghosts sweat and work out
Beside me,
Swinging
Their helpless arms
Into the sky.

The Inheritance

What I wanted
Was to be myself again
On a Monday morning, to
Wake and wash with cold water
And soap, to dress
Swiftly and walk without
Thinking
Where I came from, who I was,
To be silent and
Saved
From the long days of myself.
It no longer mattered
If I burned, bursting,
Then catching fire. It
Was enough to have
Known the war within
Myself and to be tired—
To be sick of the
Boundaries—to have
Lived in the calendar of the
Brain where one meets
One's self each day in a talking
Mirror and says, "How long
Are you here for? When
Will the war be over?" I wanted
A sea-change, a place
Where things grew into
Secrets of color
A place I imagined of festivals,
Rocks, brilliant
Reptiles, trees
And serious things—wind bells
That chime—a place

Where I could be useful.
We moved, quite suddenly,
To the Colony.
I saw ancient women
In their tennis suits
Playing all afternoon. Their men
Played Business, Journalist,
General—others were
Involved in Domestic Monopoly—
And some played
Sailor on the sea. I lived
In their fashion,
Going in and out of the
Moments. If it were not
For the fish
And melons,
For the queer atonal
Music and water slipping
In the cracks of houses,
Olive fresh-water snakes,
The strangeness—
I might have
Become a part of the Colony,
Seeing myself in that life
In which all things
Are at the height of themselves.
I might have eaten mangoes,
Had my picture taken,
Written postcards to friends
Announcing my recreation, gone
On gaping at bar-girls
And bargains, and having
Coats made by
Overnight tailors.
But I must tell you this:
One morning I woke up

And entered life;
I ran quite swiftly through the mountains,
Passing the palm trees and civets,
Watching harvests
And children
All in the ripeness of summer. It
Was then
I inherited joy
The way one inherits a fortune.

This Afternoon

The
White bird
Circles over me
Wearing a crown. He
Must have escaped
From a country where
Chinaberries dangled
From the green trees
Against yellow
Skies, where ebony spleenworts
And branches
Were dazzled by the wind
And where
His great crown
Was made. O bird! I exhale
And inhale your secrets—my
Heart beats now like
Yours
As I lead you home alive.
I am quiet
As I move through
The twigs as if they were
Clouds—I am what
I always was—a child
Leading
Birds out of the sun.
The weeds are quiet now. I
Listen to imaginary
Woods and grasses—gullies,
Trees, ponds—
None are as real

As your white pearl feathers
As we fly
Through the parables of
Trees while I call to you "Bird! Bird!"
Crying again
To be so young.

Notes on Our Life Here

We wake. Our day
Starts on the Peak: we are
Singing and burning
Our secrets. All night
We turned in the same sheets
And now we share the day.
We dress, lace our shoes, run
To find the end
Of each long walk. There is none.
Up on this high wild hill
The dangling birds
Open black fringed umbrellas
And bob
Invisible through fog—blackbird
Umbrellas,
Shielding gods.
How free,
How easy, our life
Here. There's not
Much to do
But read or answer
The doorbell. Our
Long talks,
Like water blending into
Water, have
No end—and no
Start.
Old loneliness
Goes flying with
Birds down
The green hill.
I have achieved a life that is natural.

The Central Market

Women peel
Thousand-year-old eggs
By scraping off mud
From the colored shells. Under
Great fish heads bleeding
On a string, we
Are discovered walking
Hand in hand
In this market where
Everything's possible.
We have arrived
In this human place
Of sea-horse medicine
Where sugared kumquats
Shine in glass jars
And spiders and rats
Parade through vegetables. Here,
In this winding street,
A lazy boy
Holds Chinese oranges
Inside his hands
And spends all morning
With a rubber stamp stamping
Them "Sunkist" so
They'll sell for more. Here we
Touch elephant horn—black
Tusks and ivory—
Here we touch thin private scrolls
And rims of porcelain,
See wizards carve flowers
In white mah-jongg cubes. My
Senses open wide
And make me dizzy. Waterbugs

That will refuse to drown
Burn on our sandals. Vendors
Show their teeth
Of golden stones. Suddenly, ducks,
Pressed with sleepy eyes,
Hang over us like rows
Of tennis racquets. Snakes
Are pulled out of
Baskets to be eaten. And the sun
Presses against us. Starting
From where we are,
Let's go down, down, down under cabbage and
Ginger, let us escape
These ducks and taste our lives. Under
The blood of animals
Let's turn our own lives inside out,
Throwing away petals
We cannot hold—
Families, deaths, marriages—
Discarding our histories,
Those exits and entrances
We cannot explain, mistakes,
Odd people, countries
We have slept with,
Throw ourselves
Down under dragonflies, broccoli,
Under the pythons, crushed medicines,
Spices,
While our silly tongues scratch,
Our new bodies touch,
And we are always ready to be born.

Written at Vivian Court

Shadows
Forget
Who I
Am.
I have bathed
For the second time
Today and I feel
New. Terry-cloth
Bathrobes
Bloom
In hooked
Corners, curling
Fans and brushes
Sleep in the living room,
Flowers
Burn
Holes in the air
With nude
Colors. And rain
Strikes like
Pebbles
All day,
Forming wide circles
On the window.
All morning
I have been
Thinking
Of the organization
Of paradise—the
Wide circles of planets
Forming curls

In the sky, the
Rings, stars, and heavens
Ending
In the eye of a rose.
I see myself
Tremble in
A glass of water. I
No longer know
Who I am—or who
I will be—and no
Longer care. I am changed
By thoughts
Of this morning
And changed by the
Strong
Calm of my life. Green
Whiskered birds
Fly under my
Fingers—all urgent
Messengers
Telling what I
Know. Now kingfishers
Fly through
Trees seeing
Me through the windows,
Their wings
Tough as fish scales,
Their beaks
Tougher than yellow fruit. This
Is not all. How
Can this be all
And be so true? I
Breathe my whole life
In one morning. My room

Is balanced on a cloud,
Houses below. Mad white
Pagodas tilted in brick. Long
Walks that end in
Palms. I tremble
All day
In a glass
Of water.

The Goldfish Wife

It is Monday morning
And the goldfish wife
Comes out with her laundry
To shout her message.
There! Her basket glistens
In the sun and shines—
A wicker O. And see how
The goldfish wife touches
The clothes, her fingers
Stretching toward starch,
The wind beating her hair
As though all hair
Were laundry. Come,
Dear fishwife, golden
In your gills, come tell
Us of your life and be
Specific. Come into our lives—
Where no sun shines and no
Winds spill
The laundry from the rope—
Come on the broomstick of a
Widow-witch, fly
From the empty clotheslines
Of the poor
And teach us how to air
Our lives again.

At Repulse Bay

All beaches are the same.
This was the landscape
Of my girlhood. I belonged
To great arrivals at hotels,
My uncle's girls,
The women's tennis matches,
Snarls in the nurse's wool
As she knitted me sweaters.

Why unwind the dead?
Say I was one
Who looked for the world
Beneath the blue
Sand-bucket, who searched
All day for China
In the sand. I
Waited for
Blue magic ships,
Billowing sails,
To come point-blank,
God, and discover me.

Kowloon

There was an old woman,
She walked in the street
Cawing to the bedsheets like a bird that
Is heard all morning,
That is always heard.
"What is the strange disorder
Of my past?" Shiny
Bronze tea leaves junked in a kitchen glass—
The gold horn separating wall from floor,
The horned serpent coiled around the door,
Voices of our own throats
                         in the door
Chattering, chattering.

Lantao Island

It is Sunday
On Lantao Island.
We travel by burro,
Riding into
Wave after wave of the sun.

I ride on terrible,
Soft fur, babbling
To my ancestor:
"Great-
Grandfather, hero,
You carried children
On your back, I am told,
To chauffeur them
To school
Outside a village in Austria.
To what school? And in
What village?"
A human mule.

The Asian sun is cruel.
A white straw hat
Flapping in my face
Its broken zero.

Great ancestor, hero!
You, setting out
From your village,
Your toes
And ankles
Cackling with
Chickens
In the splashing

Mud, your neck bent forward,
And on your back a
Small girl,
A student,
Saying in her perfect German,
"Hurry up, old man, giddiyup,
Go.

I ride slowly
On Lantao Island, struck silent
By changes.

The Swimming Pool

Open me. Close me,
Shout the dangerous women
Sitting around the pool doing nothing.
Open me up, they are saying, their
Lips great pocketbooks
With shiny clasps. Inside the lobby
Ancient tourists sit
Dressed in nylon, talking
Lip to lip.

Under the secret flaps
Of beach cabanas
Ideograms pour over the
Women. Old numbers, letters
Fall on their hair and nails
As light lives in the pool.

Love Song for a Jelly Fish

How amazed I was, when I was a child,
To see your life on the sand.
To see you living in your jelly shape,
Round and slippery and dangerous.
You seemed to have fallen
Not from the rim of the sea,
But from the galaxies.
Stranger, you delighted me. Weird object of
The stinging world.

Conversation of Poets

That was China! Where blue
Tiles spanned half the world—blue
Feathers hammered
By the sun. Poets wise
As Solomon
Whispering in the gardens,
Walking between gold pebbles,
Quiet, joyful, practical men.
Not one of them could be labeled mad.
All in another lifetime,
Great marble lions chiseled
And refined by water. I envy
Those poets—not their king. He
Was another thing—as we can
Imagine—seeing the broken
Columns of his city and
His clothes,
Now strands of dust sealed
Inside museums. They said,
In those days, "Poets
Are our kings—we'll bury
Them in tombs larger
Than homes!"

I envy their affection,
Brilliant as colors,
Their light-headed kindness
To each other. They took
Long walks and held each
Other, fingers clasped in the open gardens.
In their gardens

They exchanged new songs
And secrets.
Time was on their side
As they placed silk caps
Upon their black and glittering hair
And walked out, proudly, in
Their sun.

Above Sea Level

Taking root on this abandoned peak, we
No longer remember how to fall from brightness,
No longer plunder the ocean's depth
Where all is pure violence. Living new lives
Above sea level, we have forgotten
Undersea landscapes.
Tidal zones fall like towers
At the ocean's rim.
The sea divides itself into three realms:
The Zone of the Shallow Seas, the Zone of Light,
And, beneath that, the end of the sea—
That secret and silent Zone of Perpetual Darkness. These
Zones are no longer our concern.
Slowly we came to this gentle place,
Walking past stones, trees,
Dry earth, shacks, layers of garbage,
And were stared at
By hill people. They dared us to take
Root in the earth, dared us to break
Like new flowers without stalks. They saw us
Ascending.

Once water was necessary. We farmed the sea,
Hauling out food
From salinity. Mud, fish
Gave us our lonely lives. Waves and the tides—
Starfish, scallops,
Crabs, mussels, sea pork,
Rockweeds, and shells sharp as razors—
Gave us our living.
Now we no longer dream of sea palms,
Our memories have burned out sharks,

The feeding frenzy of killers.
We have ascended through sea weather
To the top of this mountain. Here grass
Blows in green waves,
Light falls on our mouths like rain, and
Nets of white clouds tighten around our lives. We
Are free of the extremity of the sea! Free
To live with our calm self-nature. Now—
Farewell to bleeding whales,
Oil-bearing targets for whalers' harpoons.
Our net is tightened. If we leave now,
It is not for the sea—but for the endless path
That will raise us even higher
Above sea level.

Climbing Victoria Peak

Down below,
Doormen, giant Sikhs
Wearing their guns and red robes,
Open glass doors to hotels
Where the new T'ang exotics—
Fruits, drugs, perfumes,
Aromatics, jewels,
Silks—are
Bartered, gathered, sold,
Nude tourists
Fitted for their suits of gold
As we leave
The city. Taking the longest path
Past furs, the Shanghai Bank
And sauna baths, we climb green
Water-steps and ferns
To reach our own hills
In the afternoon. Wasps
Motor like new cars
Through ferns. Here are
The cockroach and the cricket,
Here's the moth
Going to battle for one day on earth.
All the insects
Of the hills
Will slide
Into their golden bottles.

Oh for the butterfly changes!
Is it now possible
For us to fly? Grow into
Something new,
Deep in the order of nature
Close to the soul?

Night Harbor

Standing on
Sheila's terrace
During a party,
I'm out here alone,
Lost all evening
In the tides
Of childhood,
Drowning on
Riverside Drive
While lights
Blur in salt tears
And tug horns
Sound
As all the
Boats converge.
Sheila's terrace
Faces the China Sea
Where small hooked lights
Are strung around ships
So we can follow
The dots. From here
I can observe
Mountains and Chinese
Islands move
Like overstuffed chairs
Shifting places
In the shadows.
I want to leave this
Terrace, sit down,
And weep. Not for
The islands of Asia
That bob up and down,
Or for the boats

That give off a smell of
Plunder,
But weep for the sky I am
Under as I stand
In darkness
Towing in my life
From the other side,
The dark side
Of my eye.

Letter to Last Year

I have discovered that people lose shape,
Drop limbs and flesh and arteries
Until they are no longer blood, but, more than that,
They become pure feeling. And that is what I am
In these rooms missing you: a person lifted out
Of time and space, taking part in a voyage
That I call this "letter." How strange
To join ends with beginnings! To remember
Departures the way one remembers a dream. Year, we
Have launched our
Separations
And must wait to know
Where we are going.
We have nothing in common now
But the sense of floating
Over countries, mountains, beyond boundaries,
Into each other
Like a piece of blue steel—
That is what memory is—stronger than flesh,
A floating needle, a pen, or a ship
With an endless cargo.

Visiting Buddha

Outside

Walking around. The temple,
Quiet as a hospital.

I wanted to make a shuffling
Sound with my feet. I wanted to find

My shoulders. I wanted to look
At my toes—more than that,

Get strangers to walk with me.

I wanted to make clicking noises
Into the faces of unknown stockings and shoes,

And I wanted
To make short circles with my feet.

Inside

The stupas are curling as mad
As ice cream,
And the long, golden Buddha
Is candy king
In this temple.

In this temple of candy
The long, sleeping Buddha reclines. He's
Thinking of nothing. He's longer
Than any god. His toes

Take up the entire
Lower temple.

Always the dreamer is lost
As if he must be, to please us,
A blown-up balloon. Now

The shrimp priests
Bow to the giant's toe

And compare their own
Size to his. Why did they build the temple
Around the king?
They should have let him sleep in
The street near the trees.

Patience

On Victoria Peak
Prickly plants
Take precedence
Over tulips and roses,
And this is why
I prefer them
To flowers.
In knots of thorns,
The outward
Petals change into
Spinal forms,
Where blood
Turns back
At the flower
Edge.
Here everything beautiful
Can be dried and saved:
Pine cones, artichokes, thistles
All go on with their own
Silent and
Often uninteresting
Adornments,
But they seem to
Be hinting,
"Watch me. I will
Not fade."

The Love Singer

He appeared
Without a shadow,
Crying *joy* in a language that
We had forgotten or never knew
As syllables dropped like kumquats
From his tongue and he smiled at boys
In the street who made fun of him. He
Did not seem "Western"—he was too mad for
That, jangled and put together in a shabby way
That might have embarrassed us. And from
What place in the East he had arrived we could
Not tell—he seemed to have shed his origin
The way flowers shed petals
Until only the stem remains. And he was
That stem. Thin, made of sunlight, his face burned
By wind (all the streets he had been to!),
And he wandered
Past gaps, white buildings,
Glassy windows bursting with
Jewelry, past flowers,
Mirrors—
And what he sang was again this word *joy*
Sounding so much like a bird
Calling to his invisible mate
As he flies beyond the New Territories,
Then dips into a mountain.

Love Singer! Perhaps he once played at being
A bard in China before
Singing
In our parking lots, gardens, traffic, new
Hotel lobbies. And we listened.
And I keep asking,

"What is his name?" and
"What does he sing?" and
"What do you call that stringed
Instrument, which seems to be cared for and polished
By feathers?" Here
In this city,
Every day we have seen this miracle-monger
Walking the streets. But only once
Did I hear him speak to me clearly.

The Potential Prisoner

The backstage of this airport
Was unfamiliar. We sat
In the cubicle of the chief customs official
On broken wicker stools, staring
At framed portraits of great
Asian smugglers and close-ups
Of bizarre smuggling techniques.
I saw huge photos of men's shoes: the
Toes had pockets filled with opium. I saw
Suitcases with false tops.
Stowaway techniques are amazing; the pictures
Were so odd they made us smile.
Meanwhile, the potential prisoner
Never arrived. We drove back
To familiar things in this strange city,
To spend the night
Exchanging new information
Leading to the capture
Of our secret selves. Why should we
Hide our own lies
In the toes of our shoes?
Later, we knew
We had arrived,
Without knowing why
At that moment of revelation
When we threw out
The puffs and padding of
Our inner lies. Love,
After all, descends in the foreign dark,
Apparently praying to be caught.

The Spy

At home for a week I have been spying on fruit.
In the immense bowl the fruit has ripened
And begins to change. The colors darken at
Their edges and turn black. New shapes
Explode and warp—adding new odors
To our rooms. Sap falls out of their skins,
And, at a certain point, they change
Their shape entirely, becoming both
Substance and sap. They are so
Magically changed
When they have been in a room too long. I watch
These shapes changing from green to a darker
Green—yellow into black, orange into
Black, as if all bright colors must go, finally,
Into darkness, burst, or turn to seed.
I wonder if
All trees
Are offering only a pure excuse for words—as if
Language itself were falling
From the trees, apples
No more than the boundaries of words. Ripeness. Language.
Metamorphosis. This is what I am spying on, sitting
Patiently with silent flies,
Watching these forms of life turn mad and giddy.
Mangoes, custard apples turn, unbend,
And all become something else.
If only there were a perfect word
I could give to you—a word like some artichoke
That could sit on the table, dry, and become itself.

Three Love Poems

Crows, pheasants, cuckoos, toucans
Crawl out of everything
With faces I once loved
In my wilderness.
In this new day turning
I arrive
Where guava and fish
Hang in the sun like flies.
In this green waking
A crab,
Crawls over my eyes. Now, whatever I am,
I will always be,
And if it is death to love
I shall love a thousand times over,
Being born a thousand times
In this new day, in this new day turning,
When falcons and dogs return
To their homes in the golden grass burning,
And hawfinch and jellyfish
No longer whistle or sting.
I walk out of dreaming
Brushing off old loves like leaves—
Forgetting where I have been
For my new life's sake.

2.

Mammals fall out of the sky—
Musk shrews and porcupines
Shadow us as we sigh
To be alive in this time
When we know
What it means not to mean anything.
You, for example, are
The dragonfly,
And I, in the dark, sleep
With you each night
In this gray cocoon
Located on a mountain. Here
It is timeless. Here
It is cool. We
Never hesitate
To be silent. Or say
What we both already know: each day
Transparent lilies
Trumpet our life. Mountains
Breathe, offering burning leaves and trees.
All reptiles celebrate:
Skinks and terrapins
With bright blue tails,
Green snakes and cobras,
Corals and kraits, white
And golden, climb into our mornings,
When we run out of reason
And follow, like insects
In our innocence, watermarks
Of each miracle.

3.

This morning we picked
Birds of paradise whose wings
Were stalks,
Limbs and bones
Of mad flowers.
In the sun
This morning we could rise
To pick the wild
Planned birds of paradise.

Sea.
The palms
Shine in the night
So they now seem
To be burning
A line in the
Sky. Don't forget
The moon
Or telling
Time by the
Sea. Am I
Bent on a life-change?

The Storm

In one night
And one morning
That seemed like forty
Days and forty nights,
The raindrops came—louder
And louder—breaking
Mountains, roofs, and
Bridges, knocking glass
Buildings into their
Foundations, winding
All birds and plants
Together, mashing
Squatters' homes
Into chicken bones,
Cracking the floating
Sampans in a splintered
Sea.

Sun-Tong, handsome "Ladies' Tailor,"
Known by some to be a lady-killer,
Travels no more on his motorbike
With his plastic sacks stuffed with
Pajamas, alterations, spindles;
Sun-Tong lies under the spools of
Rock, beneath great slabs of shale,
Drowned in a splash
Of dresses. "Sun-Tong, where were
You going in the storm?"

Everything's wrong. Phones
And wires broken. The Peak roads are gone.
There's no food except
For the tin cans hauled

Up the mountains by the bravest mules.
No school either. All the land
Is sliding. On this hill,
Children slosh near the gray hospital
To watch a helicopter drop supplies. It's still
Raining.

"We shall do what we like in the rain!" think
The children, innocent of death,
As they dance into kingdom come in
Their new galoshes, splashing
Near landslides, slipping away
From their houses, dancing
Behind the backs of buildings
While rocks fall down the mountains
And the world flows. Storms
Open the dark rooms
Of Heaven—
Everything drops out
Of clouds in buckets,
Bells ring, time
Stops, and
The Wind Gates chime.

Secrets

He dreams every
Night of green
Women. In our sleep
We walk and move
About as if we were
Wrestling with
Perfect errors. He finds
The woman. Swiftly
I run to hide or
Slay her with
My melting fist.
Later, he opens the windows
And turns the woman
Over on her side
And holds in his arms
Her buzzing green shadows.
Again
In this night
He finds the woman
Blooming from the sky.
She grows brilliant, gold
Scales as saints once
Grew halos of fire.
As she unfolds her secret,
I wake with my senses wide open.

In the Empty Room of Perfection

Love
Opened my eyes to the amulets
Of trees—
Green leaves, falling miracles,
Falling, one by one,
On the street. In Japan we bought

White porcelain tipped into palm-eyes
And icicles, pots shaped like
Peach stones and glazed in sky blue.
We touched the rims of the world's glaze
But arrived without anything. Then

You gave me my own room without old things,
Without decorations, without paintings
That hang on the walls
Only to become new walls themselves, without
Shapes that interfere
With what I must be.

My dreams were unshaped and unpainted. I
Lived with the fantasy of the sea—shaped
Always on the verge of words. You—
Looked for emptiness the way lovers seek sleep,
Burned currencies
And seeds of your own beginnings. How easy
For us to change into fire-birds, fly
Past history, oceans, striking against the sky
With our own new wings. Now—

Shall we return where we came from?
You be the brush that strikes.
And, burning inside, still burning, I'll
Live as the flaming kiln that shapes the pot.

The New Life

Night Swimming

I remember that slow island
Where you took me, once, in Asia
Where the crabs had great shields of thick light
And carried, on their backs, worlds of their own.
We copied them.
The phosphorescent water tucked us in
That ocean where we will not be again
And phosphorescent water held us down
Like two stars spinning, binaries that bobbed
Into the mangrove waves. Green
Diamonds cut our lips and we became
Constellations, partners near the moon.
Seaweed lit our nipples as we swam
Through silvery schools of fish. I
Did the dead man's float and then I called,
"Hurry. We must return!"

The Beginning

With my fingers
I design blue mosques and temples
On the linen, trace them
On the pillows
While my child
Puffs like a pillow in my flesh
And changes to a moonstone
Or a pearl. Tonight
My marrow flowers into coral.

And, shall I dream, again, of minarets?
I live inside these temples
While the child
Grows in the great bulb of my shaking belly.
I see myself dance in the mirror's shards
Where life is ocean-heavy. Life begins—
Oh, dance with me until the ocean ends!
Once time and blood-cells bobbed like barnacles
Scratching at my heels, until
I left those cords and bones. Now
Nothing's known.
Child,
Will you float my marrow to the world
And tell them who I am? Now you
Curve gently like a baroque pearl. And
As you swim through the yolk-sac will you glide
Into this world of linen and new life?

The Eyes

Today your face
Grows rapidly.
Eyelid and
Ear shine
Under my skin
Like melons. We, roped
Together,
Float
In the universe
And one root
At a time, one
Vein at a time, we
Shift and I sleep
As your new eyes
Begin.

The Hands

White sprouts
Are opening. Are they
The new, soft hearts
Of peonies? ginger lilies?
Under my stone sea-snail
Belly, under that place
Of snow and sunlight,
Ivory anemones
Blow up inside me
And mushroom in the billows
Of my flesh. I ask myself
About the grace of fingers.
Fingernails,
Like bleeding-hearts,
Grow under stones. I wake
And listen to what they
Have to tell me: "We are dumb
White flowers
Under the foreign side
Of the moon.

Love Song to the Unborn

Where the spinal cord gets hooked up to the past,
Where ancient loves
Get married, drowned, or lost,
I hook with the starfish.
Our joy is without spine. I rake
The faces out like clams
And wake, turning in pain.

Late summertime. My back
Is well again. How strange
Now to be able to lift things
Or open windows. I must unbend
And throw off blankets,
Unfold by the sea.

Now, by the beach, my toes
Are white roots inside water.
When it rains
I wait for the sun,
Snoozing inside the damp sheets
On this farm
When it is warm.

I lie on my back, flat on a pumpkin field,
My flesh puffed like a gourd,
The marigolds twined around my thighs.

Find me in the deep splash
Of pumpkins, squash,
And green leaves that prickle.
I rub my fingers on the skin
Of squash—skin white as papyrus,

Smoother than porcelain—
And look up at the sun.
I know that its strength will be your own.

Here tangled yellow flowers
Pinch like fingers.
You will be here next summer,
Singing of pumpkins in your ripe spine time.
Love, I take down this landscape in my mind.

The First Meeting

I shall meet you at
The instant of your birth
When you emerge from the red leaves,
Dripping from the sea shells in my skin.

You have been swimming, too,
Against the salt weeds
Under the red leaves.

Then I shall meet you,
See you, and tell you how many mornings
Of my life

I have been sleeping
Under the flame-trees,
My veins splayed

Like the veins of leaves
Reaching beyond me
And caught in the air.

For I have always
Wanted to be born, to be
Reborn each morning,

And in your beginning
I find my own meaning.

What shall I say, what
Shall I tell you

When I meet you
For the first time?

We shall meet
Face to face
In the great, burning

New-leaf beginning,
Your first
Red leaf
Moment, then,
Of life.

A Handbook of the Heavens

I believed in you
Because you were
A stargazer. You
Began to study the heavens
While other children
Skated on smooth pavements,
"Ice cream"
In our roller-skate jargon.
While we rolled on ball bearings,
Searching
For a wide space to glide on,
You got your direction
From the sky

I know you. You loomed
In the sky
With your knees
Scraped by planets,
Went skating among
The fixed stars.
There were no neighbors
In your solar system.
You measured
Mercury, Saturn, landing
On Jupiter.
You found the blazing
Points of light terrible,
And returned to us, saying, "Mercury
Is an interesting but
Forbidden planet." You saw
Me bleed as I fell down,
Skating with my own key,
On skates sun-fast sun-slow.